Legal Malpractice in Ohio

How to Determine If Your Lawyer Committed Malpractice and What to Do About It

Slater & Zurz LLP, Attorneys at Law
Serving Clients Throughout Ohio
Office Locations:
Akron • Canton • Cleveland • Columbus

Legal Malpractice in Ohio
By: Slater & Zurz LLP
Attorneys at Law

©Copyright 2018 by Slater & Zurz LLP

All rights reserved. This book or any portion thereof may not be reproduced or used in any manner whatsoever without the express written permission of Slater & Zurz LLP.

Printed in the United States of America

First Printing 2015

For permission to reproduce or to order additional copies of this book, contact Slater & Zurz LLP by calling 1-800-297-9191 or visit our websites:

slaterzurz.com
ohiolegalmalpracticelaw.com

Table of Contents

Introduction   1

Chapter 1   5

What is Legal Malpractice?

Chapter 2   7

Examples of Legal Malpractice

Chapter 3   10

What Does Not Constitute Legal Malpractice?

Chapter 4   14

How Can You Prove Legal Malpractice?

Chapter 5   18

Damages Recoverable from Legal Malpractice

Chapter 6   20

Legal Malpractice Statute of Limitations

Chapter 7 23

Twelve Questions to Ask Before Filing a Legal Malpractice Claim

Chapter 8 26

How Do I File a Legal Malpractice Case?

Chapter 9 28

What Type of Legal Malpractice is Most Common?

The Authors 31

Introduction

Individuals and businesses place an enormous amount of trust in lawyers to handle matters that have significant consequences affecting both their lives and their futures. And overwhelmingly, most lawyers are indeed competent, professional, ethical people who live up to the trust placed in them.

Unfortunately, sometimes lawyers who are hired to look out for your best interests make major errors which lead to bad outcomes that negatively impact lives. The American Bar Association has found a common mistake made by lawyers in these instances is a failure to know or properly apply the law.

After such an experience, your trust in lawyers may be damaged and you may not feel that *another* lawyer can be trusted to go after someone in the same profession.

At Slater & Zurz LLP, we adhere to the highest level of standards and professionalism. Many Ohio lawyers and law firms will not in fact hold other lawyers accountable for their wrongful actions. Slater & Zurz LLP is not one of those firms.

For more than 40 years, our firm has helped victims who have been wronged and injured by others. We will not hesitate to take aggressive action against any lawyer who has caused a client to suffer losses and damages because of legal malpractice.

Legal malpractice occurs when a lawyer has damaged a client by performing in a negligent manner or failing to do something he or she should have done in the case or transaction.

In most instances, a former client suing his or her lawyer for legal malpractice must demonstrate that "but for" the misconduct of the attorney, the outcome of the case would have been more favorable to the client.

Of course, every case is unique, and the details associated with each situation are different. But why not make an appointment to discuss what happened to you?

It will provide you with the feedback you need to decide whether you have a legal malpractice claim that should be pursued. Rest assured, the meeting and its details will be kept confidential.

To further ease your mind, Slater & Zurz LLP offers free initial consultations. Should we agree to accept your case, it will be done on a contingency-fee basis, which means the firm receives a portion of any award or settlement obtained on your behalf as payment for services. If there is no recovery, you will not owe us any fees.

This book will explain what constitutes legal malpractice and what generally is not considered to be negligent behavior for Ohio lawyers. It explains the time limits involved in filing such a case, and the elements you must show to prove legal malpractice.

It also suggests some vital questions you should ask before deciding to pursue a legal malpractice case, and explains how to move forward in filing a legal malpractice claim if you decide to do so.

Additionally, there is information regarding the damages you can claim as a malpractice victim, and the importance of finding a malpractice lawyer who has handled similar cases.

A primary aim of the book is to help you realize that there are lawyers who are willing to help you take on another member of their profession who has caused you harm—perhaps seriously disrupting your life.

You do not have to be afraid to file suit against someone because he or she is a lawyer. Lawyers must meet many standards in their practice of the law and can be made to pay if they fail to live up to those standards.

DISCLAIMER

The information contained within this book is for informational use only. It is not intended to be used as legal advice nor should it be considered as legal advice. Furthermore, no attorney-client relationship has been formed or established because of receiving, purchasing or reading this book.

Cases involving legal malpractice are unique, complex, and involve many different legal issues where the outcome is dependent on the particulars of that specific case.

If you decide to pursue a legal malpractice case, you should consult with a qualified Ohio lawyer who has experience with legal malpractice cases in the state.

And if you would like a free consultation with an attorney at the Ohio law firm of Slater & Zurz LLP, please call 1-800-297-9191 or visit slaterzurz.com to learn more and send a message from the website.

Chapter 1
What is Legal Malpractice?

A lawyer is required to exercise the degree of care, skill and diligence that an attorney of ordinary skill and knowledge would exercises in a particular area of law. If he or she does not exercise the required level of care, the lawyer may have committed legal malpractice.

Legal malpractice occurs when a lawyer damages a client—financially or by impairing an important right—by a negligent action or lack of action. This can happen when the lawyer simply does not perform as an attorney of ordinary skill and knowledge would have performed; when the lawyer fails to fulfill obligations assumed under a fee agreement; or when the lawyer has a conflict of interest that is not disclosed to the client. Malpractice may also occur when a lawyer commits fraud or another intentional act in the course of representing a client, impairing the client's interests.

In most instances, a person suing for legal malpractice must demonstrate that "but for" the misconduct of his or her former lawyer, the outcome of the case would have been more favorable to the client. In some cases, when the lawyer fails to inform the client of a proposed settlement in a civil case, or plea deal in a criminal case, the client has to prove that the lawyer's misconduct caused the client to miss a "lost opportunity"—*i.e.*, an opportunity to obtain an outcome that would have been more favorable to the client.

A legal malpractice case consists of three components: (1) an attorney-client relationship giving rise to a duty owed by the lawyer to the client; (2) a breach of that duty—i.e., the lawyer's failure to fulfill that duty; and (3) harm to the client resulting directly from the lawyer's breach.

In other words, the client must show that the lawyer did not act in the way a lawyer of ordinary skill and diligence would have acted in similar circumstances, which resulted in provable harm—a financial loss or the loss of an important right—to the client.

Chapter 2
Examples of Legal Malpractice

There are many ways in which a lawyer can commit legal malpractice. Here are some examples:

Failure to know, research, or apply the law to the facts of the client's case;

Failure to thoroughly investigate the evidence pertaining to the client's case or to hire the proper experts;

Failure to respond to motions, attend court hearings, or comply with court orders;

Failure to file necessary documents or serve required papers;

Failure to file a lawsuit in a timely manner, or to comply with court-imposed deadlines;

Failure to sue all parties from whom the client may recover damages;

Failure to develop and implement a viable case strategy or to properly present the client's case at trial;

Failure to disclose any potential conflicts of interest and act in accordance with the client's wishes when possible; and

Failure to inform the client of any proposed or potential settlement in a civil case or a proposed plea bargain in a criminal case, and to advise the client of the pros and cons as opposed to going forward with a trial.

Settlement and Legal Malpractice

The question of settlement may come up more than once during any case—at the beginning, in the middle, or even while the trial is in progress. Once a case has been settled, the client will most likely be bound by that settlement with no opportunity to return to court if it later turns out that the settlement was unfair or unreasonable.

Legal malpractice may result if a lawyer misrepresents the terms of a proposed settlement, fails to explain the effects of accepting or rejecting a proposed settlement, or pressures the client to accept a rushed settlement before all evidence, favorable or otherwise, has been discovered.

For example, in a divorce action, many of the opposing spouse's assets may not be known at the beginning of the case. Thus, settling a divorce action too quickly could result in legal malpractice if the client is deprived of an appropriate share of any unknown or undisclosed assets.

Similarly, in a personal injury suit, the extent of the plaintiff's injuries, or the future costs for the plaintiff's care and treatment, may not be known in the early stages of the case. Whether the client will be able to work again may not be known. Legal malpractice may result if the lawyer pressures the client into a premature settlement that does not adequately provide for the client's needs.

Legal malpractice may also result if a lawyer accepts or rejects a proposed settlement without the client's informed consent.

Chapter 3
What Does Not Constitute Legal Malpractice?

If your lawyer lost your case or failed to keep you informed about aspects of it, or even was late to every scheduled court date, this does not mean that he or she has committed legal malpractice. If the outcome of your case would have been the same despite the actions of your lawyer, or you cannot prove that the outcome would have been more favorable to you, legal malpractice probably has not occurred.

To proceed with a malpractice case, you must meet these requirements:

An attorney-client relationship must have been established;

Your lawyer must have breached the required duty of reasonable care owed to you by acting or failing to act;

Your lawyer's breach of duty must have been a direct cause of damage or injury to you;

You must have suffered actual injury, loss, or damage.

It is important to note that the issue of professional misconduct by a lawyer can be a separate matter from legal malpractice.

A lawyer is required to act in accordance with ethical standards listed and described in the Ohio Rules of Professional Conduct. For violating these rules, a lawyer can be sanctioned by the Ohio Supreme Court. Sanctions range from a public reprimand to permanent disbarment, prohibiting the lawyer from ever practicing law in Ohio again. While other states are not required to impose similar sanctions on an Ohio lawyer, other states typically will take the Ohio lawyer's disciplinary status into consideration.

In conjunction with a lawyer's disciplinary case, the lawyer may be required to pay former clients money he or she wrongfully took or received from them. However, a disciplinary action based on a violation of the Rules of Professional Conduct is not the same as—and should not be seen as a substitute for—a legal malpractice action.

A disciplinary action is focused on the lawyer's misconduct, and will not address all the damages the client suffered. It is only through a legal malpractice action that the client may be made "whole"—*i.e.*, compensated for all the losses sustained as a result of the lawyer's misconduct.

If your lawyer's conduct was unethical, but did not result in a less favorable outcome in your case, the mere violation of the Rules of Professional Conduct will not, by itself, constitute malpractice. An experienced legal malpractice firm should be able to tell you whether a particular violation of the Rules of Professional Conduct would also support a malpractice claim, based on the specific facts of your case.

Here are some of the ethical requirements contained in the Rules of Professional Conduct:

To provide competent representation, requiring the skill, thoroughness and preparation necessary.

To act with reasonable diligence and promptness and to reasonably consult with the client regarding the means by which the client's objectives are to be accomplished.

To keep the client reasonably informed of developments in the case and comply as soon as possible with the client's requests for information.

To keep client matters confidential unless the client consents to information being revealed.

To disclose any perceived conflict of interest to the client.

To not represent opposing parties in the same litigation unless (1) the lawyer has fully disclosed the potential conflict of interest to the affected clients and the clients have consented; and (2) the lawyer believes his dual representation will not materially affect either party. For example, two spouses seeking to dissolve their marriage and who agree on the terms may choose to use the same lawyer to save money. If their interests later conflict while the case is pending, the lawyer may have to withdraw from representing at least one of the spouses.

To inform clients within a reasonable time after initiating representation what services the lawyer will provide and how fees will be determined. Generally, fees are determined on an hourly basis or are contingent on the result of the representation. A lawyer must state what percentage of the amount recovered will go to the lawyer in the event of settlement, trial, or appeal. The lawyer must inform the client about additional fees and costs (court filing fees, expert witness fees, etc.) which the client must pay.

Chapter 4
How Can You Prove Legal Malpractice?

A viable claim for legal malpractice requires proof that the lawyer's alleged mistakes caused actual damages to the former client. Courts will not simply assume that the outcome would have been more favorable for the client. There must be proof that the lawyer's action or inaction caused the client to receive a less favorable outcome.

You hired a lawyer because you needed to rely on a professional whom you could trust to know the law and how the legal system works. You expected your lawyer to be competent and handle your case as a professional. You did not anticipate that your lawyer would make a series of mistakes or an error so significant that there would be no way to fix things and recoup your losses.

To successfully prove legal malpractice, you must show (1) that your former lawyer owed you a duty, (2) that the lawyer breached that duty, and (3) that the breach caused you to suffer damages—most commonly, a financial loss. The burden of proving malpractice will be on you and your malpractice lawyer.

To show that your former lawyer owed you a duty, you must prove the existence of a client-lawyer relationship. This is usually the easiest element to prove, and can be shown by documents such as a fee agreement, court papers signed on your behalf by the lawyer, copies of emails, letters, and phone records. Subject to a few very limited exceptions, you cannot file a malpractice suit against a lawyer who did not agree to represent you specifically (as opposed to a co-worker, family member, etc., with the same issue as yours).

Proving a breach of duty is more difficult. Often, an expert will be required to explain what a competent lawyer would have done under similar circumstances, and what your former lawyer should have done. Your former lawyer may present an expert to support the claim that his or her conduct was reasonable.

Whether or not your lawyer breached the standard of care owed to you as a client will likely be a question of fact, with the outcome dependent on credibility. Whose version of what happened is most believable? Whose expert seems more knowledgeable concerning what your former lawyer should have done? An experienced legal malpractice firm may be familiar with top quality experts who have the background and professional expertise to persuade a jury that your lawyer's conduct was below the standard that you deserved.

Damages and causation—that you sustained damages as a direct result of your former lawyer's breach—may be the most difficult element to prove. Weaknesses in your underlying case may be raised in your malpractice lawsuit to show that you would have lost even if the malpractice had not occurred.

In many instances, you may have to prove a "case within a case." In other words, you may have to retry your underlying case all over, with your former lawyer substituted for the opposing party in the underlying case. You must demonstrate that you would have won the underlying case but for your former lawyer's malpractice.

"Attorney Judgment Rule"

Some states have adopted an "attorney judgment rule," which differs from state to state. In some states, lawyers may select any "reasonable" course of action in handling a client's case, without facing liability for legal malpractice, even if the lawyer's decision turns out to have been wrong.

The issue is whether the lawyer's judgment was within the range of reasonable alternatives. Mere errors in judgment made in good faith are not malpractice.

Ohio has not adopted this rule *per se*. However, a lawyer who exercises the degree of care, skill, and diligence expected of a reasonably competent lawyer may be found not to have committed malpractice based on a reasonable, good faith decision that impaired the client's interests.

Chapter 5
Damages Recoverable from Legal Malpractice

There are three types of damages typically sought in a legal malpractice claim: (1) compensatory damages; (2) consequential damages; and (3) punitive damages.

Compensatory damages compensate a client for the actual loss he or she has sustained as a result of the lawyer's malpractice. These damages are designed to make the former client "whole" for the loss the client suffered, or to put the client in the position he or she would have been in, had the malpractice not occurred. Compensatory damages include economic damages, and non-economic damages.

Economic damages reflect monetary losses that can be measured by a precise dollar amount, such as lost wages, medical expenses, and property that has been damaged or destroyed. Non-economic damages include emotional distress, and loss of a spouse's or child's companionship. In Ohio, non-economic damages are often subject to caps. Economic damages are not limited in this way.

Consequential damages are intended to compensate a former client for additional losses related to the malpractice, such as the attorney fees a client may incur in an effort to correct the malpractice.

Punitive damages are meant to punish the lawyer for his or her wrongful conduct and to deter similar conduct in the future by other lawyers. Punitive damages are not awarded for mere negligence in a legal malpractice action.

To recover punitive damages, the client must show that the former lawyer acted fraudulently or with malice. Punitive damages cannot be awarded unless the client is also entitled to recover compensatory damages.

Chapter 6
Legal Malpractice Statute of Limitations

In Ohio, you have a limited time in which to file a legal malpractice suit against your former lawyer. You do not have the luxury of acting when you get around to it.

A "statute of limitations" is a law that establishes the maximum amount of time during which a person can wait before filing a lawsuit. If a person files beyond the time identified in the state's statute of limitations, the lawsuit may be dismissed and cannot be refiled. Statutes of limitations vary, depending upon the nature of the case.

The law exists for the benefit of the defendant. A defendant cannot reasonably be expected to defend himself or herself after evidence has been destroyed, memories have faded, and it is difficult for the court to determine what really happened a long time ago.

In Ohio, you cannot file a legal malpractice case more than one year after (a) the time when you discovered, or should have discovered, that your interests were harmed as a result of something your lawyer did or did not do, or (b) the termination of your relationship with the lawyer concerning the case or transaction in which the malpractice occurred, whichever is later.

When the one-year period begins to run, and therefore when the limitations period expires, turns on two factual determinations: (1) When should you have known that your lawyer harmed or compromised your interests? (2) When did the attorney-client relationship end?

You may realize immediately that you have a malpractice claim when your lawyer loses your case. Other times, because the legal process is so complex, you may not discover until later what your lawyer did or did not do that might have been in error or negligent.

A full year could run from the date of discovery if you "should have discovered" you were injured because of the legal malpractice. Be aware that "should have discovered" is a term open to interpretation. It is possible the time period could be extended because of the circumstances, but do not expect this to be a guaranteed result and delay filing. This could be a big mistake.

In any event, if you think you have a legal malpractice case, you should not delay in contacting a legal malpractice lawyer.

Chapter 7
Twelve Questions to Ask Before Filing a Legal Malpractice Claim

Legal malpractice occurs when a lawyer damages his client by an improper action or failure to act. A person suing for legal malpractice must demonstrate that the lawyer's misconduct directly caused harm to the client.

If you are wondering whether you might be the victim of legal malpractice, you need to ask yourself the following questions:

1. Did my lawyer sufficiently prepare for my case?

2. Was the case dismissed because my lawyer failed to diligently pursue it?

3. Was my case dismissed because my lawyer failed to designate expert witnesses, to provide adequate expert reports, or present necessary expert testimony?

4. Was the case dismissed because my lawyer failed to file documents on time?

5. Did my lawyer conduct an adequate investigation or discovery, to learn all the important facts bearing on my case?

6. Did I lose the case because my lawyer drafted a document or agreement that was inadequate or ambiguous, or was I sued because of a defect in that document?

7. Did my lawyer wrongfully take or retain money from me or an estate with which I was involved?

8. Did my lawyer force me to settle my case for an inadequate amount due to a conflict of interest or other unacceptable reasons? Was I informed about this conflict?

9. Did my lawyer force me to settle out of court instead of going to trial because of his or her lack of preparation or experience?

10. Was the case settled without my approval?

11. Did my lawyer fail to tell me about all the possible outcomes in going forward to trial as opposed to settling my case, so that I could make an informed decision about how to proceed?

12. Did my lawyer "dump" my case just before the statute of limitations ran out, without doing anything to protect my interests?

These are just a few of the questions that might suggest your lawyer committed malpractice. If your answer to any of these questions is "yes," you may have a legal malpractice case against that lawyer. Because of the one-year time limitation imposed by the statute of limitations, you should contact a law firm experienced in legal malpractice as soon as possible. It can't hurt to inquire if you suspect you may have a case.

Chapter 8
How Do I File a Legal Malpractice Case?

The first step is to try to determine whether malpractice occurred. Second, you should retrieve your case file from the lawyer in question. The file is legally your property, and may contain correspondence, pleadings, discovery, memoranda, and research that your malpractice lawyer will need to evaluate and proceed with your case.

If you believe your lawyer committed malpractice, you should contact an established firm with a record of success in handling legal malpractice cases. It's important to do this as soon as possible so that your case can be filed before the statute of limitations runs out. Asking the malpractice lawyer for specific examples of cases his or her firm has handled in the past is just as important as inquiring about the possibilities of winning your case in the present.

If your former lawyer does not have malpractice insurance, you should have been informed of that in writing when you hired him or her. Some malpractice insurance does not cover such things as fraud, theft or willful injury. If the lawyer doesn't have full insurance coverage for malpractice, it may impair your ability to fully recover.

Be aware that in most cases, expert testimony must be presented in support of a legal malpractice claim. Ideally, you should have an expert with unimpeachable knowledge, skill, integrity, and a strong reputation. A full-service law firm that has successfully handled legal malpractice cases in the past is in the best position to select an expert who can help you win your case.

Chapter 9
What Type of Legal Malpractice is Most Common?

Many clients do not realize they have been victims of legal malpractice. They may believe their lawyer did something wrong that negatively affected the outcome of the case, but they are not certain whether they should investigate their former lawyer's actions.

Simply being unhappy with the result of your case does not mean that you are the victim of malpractice. You must prove that your former lawyer did not act in the way a diligent, reasonably competent lawyer would have acted under the circumstances. You will also need to show that you suffered harm, and that the lawyer's conduct was responsible.

Every few years the American Bar Association (ABA) Standing Committee on Lawyers' Professional Conduct ranks the most common legal malpractice claims by type in the United States and Canada. These studies include data from many insurers and thousands of legal malpractice claims.

As reported by the ABA, malpractice claims related to real estate spiked after the most recent recession. By 2016, these claims were subsiding. This was accompanied by an uptick in the number of estate, trust, and probate claims, probably attributable to rising numbers of retiring baby boomers and disputes over the estates of aging families.

The most common complaint that resulted in the filing of a legal malpractice case involved the lawyer's failure to know or apply the law. This type of malpractice may occur when the lawyer doesn't know the law, or when the lawyer researches the law but doesn't recognize the applicable principles. It may also occur if the lawyer knows the law but uses incorrect reasoning. Finally, this type of malpractice may occur when the lawyer ignores the clear legal implications of known facts.

Planning errors—poor strategy or judgment concerning how to handle a case—are the second most common basis for legal malpractice claims. Planning errors may occur when the lawyer knows the law and the facts. A lawyer's failure to fully investigate all facts bearing on the outcome of the case is the third most common reason behind the filing of malpractice suits.

Other causes that lead to the filing of legal malpractice cases include a lawyer's failure to file documents on time, failure to know or comply with deadlines, procrastination, failure to obtain the client's consent when appropriate, conflicts of interest, and fraud.

The Authors

The Ohio law firm of Slater & Zurz LLP is a team of legal professionals dedicated to helping victims of all types of accidents as well as their families.

The law firm has been entrusted with more than 30,000 personal injury cases since its founding and has helped clients receive more than $150 million in settlements and verdicts.

Attorney Jim Slater is the managing partner of Slater & Zurz LLP and has been actively practicing law for more than 40 years. When Jim is asked what his law firm does, he replies simply by saying:

"We Make Others Do What They Do Not Want to Do."

We make the decision makers at insurance companies pay fair and proper compensation to victims of accidents.

We make individuals and businesses pay their customers and employees the money they owe them.

We provide comfort to families by legally pursuing owners and operators of nursing homes that harm their loved ones.

We convince juries to award our clients the money they deserve.

In all cases, we work tirelessly to be sure our clients get what they are entitled to receive.

Prior to asking for our help, our clients were either denied proper compensation or were uncertain whether they could receive the compensation they deserved.

We have made companies pay millions when they negligently manufactured products that caused serious injuries.

We have made insurance companies pay hundreds of thousands of dollars when the dogs of homeowners they insured attacked innocent children and caused serious injury.

We have made a hospital pay millions when one of the doctors they employed caused a child's death.

We made a large company pay millions to its employees when they failed to pay them commissions they rightfully earned.

At Slater & Zurz LLP, all our cases do not involve millions or hundreds or thousands of dollars. Many involve smaller amounts of money, to be sure. But there is a common theme. We make companies and people who treat our clients unfairly do what they do not want to do.

This is what we do at Slater & Zurz LLP. This is what we have done for more than 30,000 clients over 40 plus years. I am personally proud of the difference we make for our clients.

It has been our goal from the beginning to make our clients proud that we are representing them and pleased with the results we obtain on their behalf.

- **James W. Slater**

Free Consultations Are Always Offered at
Slater & Zurz LLP
Attorneys at Law
Serving Clients Throughout Ohio
From These Office Locations:
Akron • Canton • Cleveland • Columbus

Please call toll free
1-800-297-9191
or visit slaterzurz.com

More Free Books Available from Slater & Zurz LLP

We have written books on many different legal topics including the following:

When A Dog Bites Fight Back

Stop Nursing Home Abuse in Ohio

Motorcycle Crashes in Ohio

Trucking Accidents in Ohio

A Wrongful Death in Ohio

To request a free copy of any of our books, please call 1-800-297-9191 or send us a message from our website at slaterzurz.com.

www.ingramcontent.com/pod-product-compliance
Lightning Source LLC
Chambersburg PA
CBHW070723180526
45167CB00004B/1598